Baltimore & Ohio Railroad
in the Potomac Valley

MARTIN J. McGUIRK

KALMBACH
BOOKS

© 2001 Kalmbach Publishing Co. All rights reserved. This book may not be reproduced in part or in whole without written permission of the publisher, except in the case of brief quotations used in reviews. Published by Kalmbach Publishing Co., 21027 Crossroads Circle, Waukesha, WI 53187.

Printed in the United States of America

00 01 02 03 04 05 06 07 08   10 9 8 7 6 5 4 3 2 1

Visit our website at http://kalmbachbooks.com
Secure online ordering available

Publisher's Cataloging-in-Publication
(Provided by Quality Books, Inc.)

McGuirk, Martin J.
     Baltimore and Ohio railroad in the Potomac
Valley / Martin J. McGuirk. — 1st ed.
     p. cm.
     Includes index.
     ISBN: 0-89024-421-9

     1. Baltimore and Ohio Railroad Company.
2. Railroads—United States. I. Title.

   TF25.B2.M34 2000   385'.0973
                              QBI00-500128
Book design: Kristi Ludwig
Cover design: Lisa Zehner

On the cover: Nearing the end of the steam movements over the Baltimore & Ohio's famed Cranberry Grade between M&K Junction and Terra Alta, West Virginia, a quartet of diesel helpers shoves (note caboose) a long coal drag up to the summit. Meanwhile, on the high iron, EM-1 no. 7608, in command of train no. 96, the St. Louis–Jersey City Time-Saver freight, charges 'round the first leg of the long S-curve through Amblersburg, W. Va. Photo by H. W. Potin, Nov. 7, 1951

Contents

Brief History of the Baltimore & Ohio

On July 4, 1828, the citizens of Baltimore, Maryland, celebrated the laying of the first stone of the Baltimore & Ohio Railroad. The last surviving signer of the Declaration of Independence, Charles Carroll, was in attendance, saying that participating in this event was second only to his actions back in 1776. The stone is still on display in the B&O Railroad Museum, located at the old Mount Clare Shops in Baltimore.

The story of the Baltimore & Ohio Railroad is really a story of firsts. Sure, there is financial intrigue, design and construction of engineering marvels, mighty locomotives, a hard lesson in the wasteful destruction of war, and fast passenger trains. But the B&O always shone as an innovator, a pioneer, a company that in many ways invented an industry.

At the same time the Baltimore & Ohio was a remarkably conservative railroad, building a reputation for reliability and service. A story of firsts—there's no better way to describe the very first common carrier railroad in the United States, and the first railroad to offer regularly scheduled freight and passenger service.

The challenges faced by the fledgling company when it received a charter on February 28, 1827, to build a railroad from Baltimore, Maryland, to a suitable point on the Ohio River are almost incomprehensible to us today. Everything, from the most efficient way to schedule trains to the very trains themselves, had to be invented.

Even the railroad's name seemed a precursor to certain failure. To proper Baltimoreans in the 1820s the Ohio River wasn't an easy drive from their fair city, but a hazardous journey through a still untamed wilderness, a few sparse settlements surrounded by danger and death. Settlers had made some inroads in the Ohio territory, but their settlements were a far cry from the civilized streets of Baltimore.

To be sure, there were railroads in England that would serve as the pattern for much of the early Baltimore & Ohio, but American railroads were different. In England railroads were built, often at great expense, between existing population centers.

In America railroads were used to open up the wilderness. The railroad came first, which meant that the line had to be built as quickly and cheaply as possible. Only when it had paid for itself were improvements forthcoming.

FIRST STONE.
of the
BALT. & OHIO RAIL ROAD

First steps

While it may still have been untamed wilderness, the State of Ohio was booming by the early 1820s and Baltimore wanted a piece of the action. After all, the city offered one of the finest natural harbors in America. Better still, Baltimore was closer to the Ohio than her two biggest rivals, Philadelphia and New York City. The problem wasn't getting the ships into Baltimore harbor, the problem was getting the goods from Baltimore inland. Both New York and Philadelphia seemed to have the answer: canals. New York's Erie Canal was opened in 1825, permitting navigation all the way to Lake Erie.

In 1826 Pennsylvania granted a charter for a system of canals to link Philadelphia with Pittsburgh. Baltimore decided against a canal for two reasons. First, the only route for the canal would be south to Washington and then along the Potomac; this would be the same route used by the Chesapeake & Ohio canal, which was already under construction. Second, a canal west from Baltimore would run into the tree-covered wall formed by the Allegheny Mountains, a difficult prospect for a canal. A railroad was deemed to be the only viable solution.

Ground was broken for the Baltimore & Ohio in a suitably elaborate ceremony on July 4, 1828. The first stone for the railroad was laid by Charles Carroll, last surviving signer of the Declaration of Independence. Carroll obviously knew the importance railroads would play in the economic growth of the country he helped found when he said, "I consider this among the most important acts of my life, second only to my signing the Declaration of Independence, if even it be second to that."

The railroad followed a course along the Patapsco and Monocacy Rivers towards the Potomac, arriving in Ellicott's Mills, the first major city west of Baltimore, on May 24, 1830. By 1853, 25 years after construction commenced, the line reached Wheeling, West Virginia (which, of course, was still Virginia until the western part of the Old Dominion became a separate state in 1863), a total of 379 miles west of Baltimore.

With a route running through the border state of Maryland and lines through Virginia, the B&O was harder hit by the Civil War than any other northern railroad. Lines were raided, bridges burned, and cars and locomotives were captured on more than one occasion. It could be said that the first shooting battle of the Civil War was fought in Harpers Ferry, years before the firing on Fort Sumpter, when abolitionist John Brown captured the arsenal there with plans to start a slave revolt. Brown and his men were captured by Colonel Robert E. Lee, the very same Lee who couldn't raise his sword against his home state of Virginia and went on to lead the Confederate army.

Westward and northward expansion

After the Civil War the B&O entered a period of expansion. In 1866 it leased the Central Ohio, a line running between Bellaire, Ohio, and Columbus by way of Wheeling. In 1869 a line between Newark and Sandusky, Ohio, was also added to the system. From a point on that line originally called Chicago Junction (later renamed Willard after Dan Willard, president of the B&O from 1910 to 1941) the B&O built a line west to Chicago, reaching the Windy City in 1874.

In 1872 the B&O leased the recently completed Pittsburgh & Connellsville Railroad, which ran between Cumberland, Maryland, and Pittsburgh, Pennsylvania. A year later the Metropolitan Branch was built north from Washington, D.C., to a connection with the main line at Point of Rocks, Md.

During the 1870s and '80s the B&O and Pennsylvania Railroad found themselves embroiled in a dispute on routes between Washington and Philadelphia. In the 1870s the two railroads, along with the Philadelphia, Wilmington & Baltimore, operated trains between Staten Island and the nation's capital. The B&O was less than cooperative about ticketing through passengers and billing freight. The Pennsy took a hard line and built a slightly roundabout route between Baltimore and Washington in 1872. This was legal, even though the B&O's charter granted monopoly on traffic between the two cities. The B&O responded by moving its New York trains off the Pennsy and onto the Philadelphia & Reading–Central Railroad of New Jersey route east of Philadelphia.

The Pennsy, never one to be trifled with, acquired control of the Philadelphia, Wilmington & Baltimore in 1881. The B&O, fighting fire with fire, proposed to build a line of its own between Baltimore and Philadelphia with its own terminal facilities on Staten Island, providing access to Manhattan via a ferry connection. In 1884 the Pennsy refused to handle B&O

trains east of Baltimore. The B&O had no choice but to complete its own line (known as the Royal Blue Line) in 1886 from Baltimore to Philadelphia, parallel to the PW&B and more than a few miles from it.

In addition to the line to Chicago the B&O served the "other" gateway to the west, St. Louis. In the late 1880s the railroad acquired control of a route between Parkersburg, W.Va., through Cincinnati to St. Louis (the original Baltimore & Ohio Southwestern, completed in 1857). The same period saw completion of a line between Akron, Ohio, and Chicago Junction to tie in with the former Pittsburgh & Western, now under B&O control, between Pittsburgh and Akron.

Hard times

The massive expansion of the 1870s and '80s left the B&O with a large, farflung system. But the financial picture was hardly bright. The railroad had a large-standing debt, revenues were low and dropping—the B&O's share of the soft coal traffic always served as a strong bellwether of the railroad's financial health. In 1889 the railroad handled 31 percent of the nation's tidewater soft coal traffic; by 1896 that number had dropped to 6 percent, a result of competition

from other railroads. In a cost-saving measure the B&O cut back on maintenance, quickly acquiring a reputation for unreliability. The inevitable followed soon after—the B&O entered receivership in 1896.

The railroad managed to emerge from receivership three years later. In 1901 the Pennsy bought a large amount of B&O stock, appointing Leonor Loree president of the road. Over the next nine years he instituted widespread physical plant improvements, reducing grades and easing curvature on many routes as well as double-tracking large sections of the line. He also acquired a large interest in the Reading, itself a major shareholder in the Central of New Jersey.

Trend-setting leadership

More than any other individual, Daniel Willard is responsible for the B&O's conservative personality which dominated throughout the first half of the 20th century. Becoming president of the railroad in 1910, Willard immediately made changes to improve the railroad. The B&O acquired the Chicago Terminal Transfer Railroad in 1910, purchased the Coal & Coke Railway (between Elkins and Charleston, W.Va.) in 1917, and acquired portions of the Cincinnati,

Hamilton & Dayton and its leased lines, forming a route between Cincinnati and Toledo.

Although not the most important event of Willard's presidency, perhaps the most memorable was the 1927 Fair of the Iron Horse, a pageant and expedition of railroad history and technological development. Held at Halethorpe, Md., the expedition featured much of the B&O's museum collection. If the original locomotives or cars were no longer in existence, replicas of historically significant rolling stock were carefully constructed. This collection forms the nucleus of the B&O Railroad Museum in Baltimore, today one of the finest facilities of its kind in the country.

In the 1920s the Interstate Commerce Commission developed a merger plan designed to improve the efficiency of the nation's railroads, eliminate redundant routes, and create regional railroads. This created a frenzy of acquisition among many railroads, including the B&O. In 1926 it purchased the Cincinnati, Indianapolis & Western's line between Hamilton, Ohio, and Springfield, Illinois. The B&O then acquired an 18 percent interest in the Wheeling & Lake Erie in 1927 and started purchasing stock in the Western Maryland that same

year. In 1929 the B&O purchased the Chicago & Alton, reorganizing it as the Alton Railroad and operating it as part of the B&O (until it gained independence for a brief period between 1943 and 1947, when it was merged into the Gulf, Mobile & Ohio). The Buffalo, Rochester & Pittsburgh entered the fold in 1932, acquired from the Van Sweringens in exchange for the B&O's interest in the W&LE. That same year the B&O purchased the Buffalo & Susquehanna.

War years and the onset of dieselization

Roy H. White was president of the Baltimore & Ohio during a decade that saw the railroad's greatest challenges and changes. Desperate to avoid the federal control that had been enforced on the railroads through the United States Railroad Administration during and immediately after World War I, the nation's railroads made every effort to cooperate with government and military officials and each other, even before the country entered World War II. Shortly after the attack on Pearl Harbor plunged the U.S. into the shooting war, President Franklin D. Roosevelt established the Office of Defense Transportation (ODT). Capably led by Joseph P. Eastman, member of the ICC and coordinator

of transportation for the federal government between 1933 and 1936, the railroads successfully met the intense demands of war shipment with little or no direct federal control. (The only exception was during brief labor difficulties in December 1943 and January 1944.)

Interestingly, the B&O, like every other railroad in the country, was faced with the need to move record amounts of traffic with considerably less equipment and people than it owned and operated in the first war. Railroads in 1941 had 31 percent fewer locomotives, 24 percent fewer freight cars, and 35 percent fewer passenger cars, as well as a work force about 24 percent smaller than they'd had in 1917. The difference was in the capability of the equipment. Technological innovations between the war, and improvements in the railroad's physical plant, were the key. That smaller work force was operating heavier locomotives with a greater tractive effort that were capable of pulling longer, faster, and heavier trains than had been possible in 1917.

The B&O did need some new equipment to handle its share of the war traffic. Material shortages meant the railroad, like all the others, didn't get everything it wanted, but there was a modest increase in the B&O's roster during the war. More than 150 locomotives were added to the roster between 1941 and '45. The largest single class of new wartime motive power were the 30 2-8-8-4 EM-1 class articulateds. With a tractive effort of 115,000 pounds, these giants tipped the scales at just over one million pounds each. Everyone on the railroad, including president White, agreed they were the ultimate in B&O motive power.

There's no denying the power and beauty of the EM-1s. But the internal combustion power authorized for delivery to the B&O during the war, consisting of a number of sets of FT freight road diesels, 40 diesel switchers, and nine passenger slant-nosed E units, was indicative of things to come. Few were able to deny the operating efficiency and high availability of the new diesel engines. Once the war ended, dieselization was merely a matter of time, but the golden era created by the combination of steam and diesel power, the availability of relatively inexpensive film and cameras, and the availability of automobile access to the right-of way, created a rush of railfans to trackside in the late 1940s and '50s and produced the photos found in this book.

The changes in the railroad industry were far-ranging between 1945 and 1965—far more than the switch from steam to diesel. Ancient freight cars, kept in service because of a lack of funds throughout the Depression and the sheer need of the war years were still around in 1945. Thirty-six-foot boxcars and short hoppers built in the first decade of the century were still in service. By 1960 those cars, and many of the "modern" 40-foot boxcars built in the 1930s, had been superseded by 50-foot boxcars and 100-ton-capacity hoppers. Even the jack-of-all-trades boxcar, which for years had been used to transport everything from automobiles to wheat, had been complemented by covered hoppers, auto racks, and other specialized cars—an economic necessity in response to higher labor costs and increased competition.

Railroading was still very much a manpower-intensive operation in 1945—tower operators and station agents played as much of a role in moving trains as engineers and conductors. By 1965 most of the "small town" railroading jobs were gone, and those that were still around were clearly on borrowed time. Perhaps most important, the railroad still was "the" way to travel or to

ship goods and raw materials in 1945. Within 20 years the railroads had clearly lost the edge to trucks, airplanes, and automobiles. By the late 1960s the handwriting was on the wall and the railroads, including the Baltimore & Ohio, knew they needed to find a new way to do things if they were going to remain in existence into the 21st century.

C&O control and Chessie

In 1960 the Chesapeake & Ohio started acquiring B&O stock, gaining control of the railroad in 1962. By 1964 the C&O owned 90 percent of the B&O stock, and by 1967 the ICC authorized the B&O and C&O to acquire control of the Western Maryland. On June 15, 1973, the B&O, C&O, and WM were made subsidiaries of the newly formed Chessie System, ending the independent corporate existence of the oldest railroad in the country, and one of the oldest in the world.

The B&O in the classic era

The years 1930 through 1960 are often referred to as the classic era among railfans and model railroaders. It was during this time the railroads saw great change—the conversion from steam to diesel motive power, modernized methods of train dispatching, traffic control,

Baltimore and Ohio Railroad Data

	1929	1972
Miles of railroad operated:	5,658	5,491
Number of locomotives:	2,364	995
Number of passenger cars:	1,732	23
Number of freight cars:	102,072	
Number of company service cars:	3,092	
Number of freight and company service cars:		56,305

Location of headquarters: Baltimore, Maryland
Reporting marks: BO
Notable named passenger trains: *Capitol Limited* (New York–Chicago), *National Limited* (New York–St. Louis), *Royal Blue* (New York–Washington), *Cincinnatian* (Baltimore–Cincinnati, later Detroit–Cincinnati)

Historical and technical society: Baltimore & Ohio Historical Society, P. O. Box 13578, Baltimore, MD 21203-3578
Recommended reading:
Impossible Challenge, by Herbert H. Harwood, Jr., published in 1979 by Barnard, Roberts & Co.
History of the Baltimore & Ohio Railroad, by John F. Stover, published in 1987 by Purdue University Press, South Campus Courts–D, West Lafayette, IN 47907 (ISBN: 0-911198-81-4)
Subsidiaries and affiliated railroads, 1972:
Baltimore & Ohio Chicago Terminal (100%)
Staten Island Rapid Transit Railway (100%)
Reading Company (38.3%)
Western Maryland (43.3%)

Washington Terminal (50%, jointly with Penn Central, formerly Pennsylvania)
Richmond-Washington Co. (16.7%)
Monongahela (33.3%)
Predecessor railroads:
Buffalo & Susquehanna
Buffalo, Rochester & Pittsburgh
Successors:
Chessie System
CSX Transportation

Excerpted from *The Historical Guide to North American Railroads,* Second Edition, available from Kalmbach Publishing Co.

---

and communications, and the development of streamlined passenger trains to replace the older conventional "heavyweight" equipment. This classic era also marks the sharp increase in competition from highways and airlines. In 1930 the automobile was making inroads on passenger travel, especially on secondary routes, but for long-distance or first-class travel the train was still the way to go. By 1960 that had changed. Automobiles and airlines had bumped rail travel into a distant third place. Most of the passenger trains that still ran were shadows of their for-

mer selves, usually kept running in order to honor government mail contracts. When the mail went to trucks and airplanes, many thought it was the death blow for passenger trains. Happily Amtrak stepped in and saved the day.

But those dark days were still in the future when the photos in this book were taken. Perhaps "in the Potomac Valley" is not the best way to describe this book; the photos span most of the eastern region of the Baltimore & Ohio, from the unmistakable skyline of Manhattan Island to the deepest hollers of Appalachia. But how else can one

describe a region so diverse?

The locales depicted in these photos show the heart of the B&O. While the B&O ranged as far afield as St. Louis and Chicago, "out there" it was a midwestern road. Only in the railroad's backyard can one find the "true" B&O, or at least the one fondly remembered by most fans of this unique transportation enterprise.

And no part of the B&O's backyard was more its heart than the valley formed by the Potomac River and tributaries. Hence the name *Baltimore & Ohio in the Potomac Valley.*

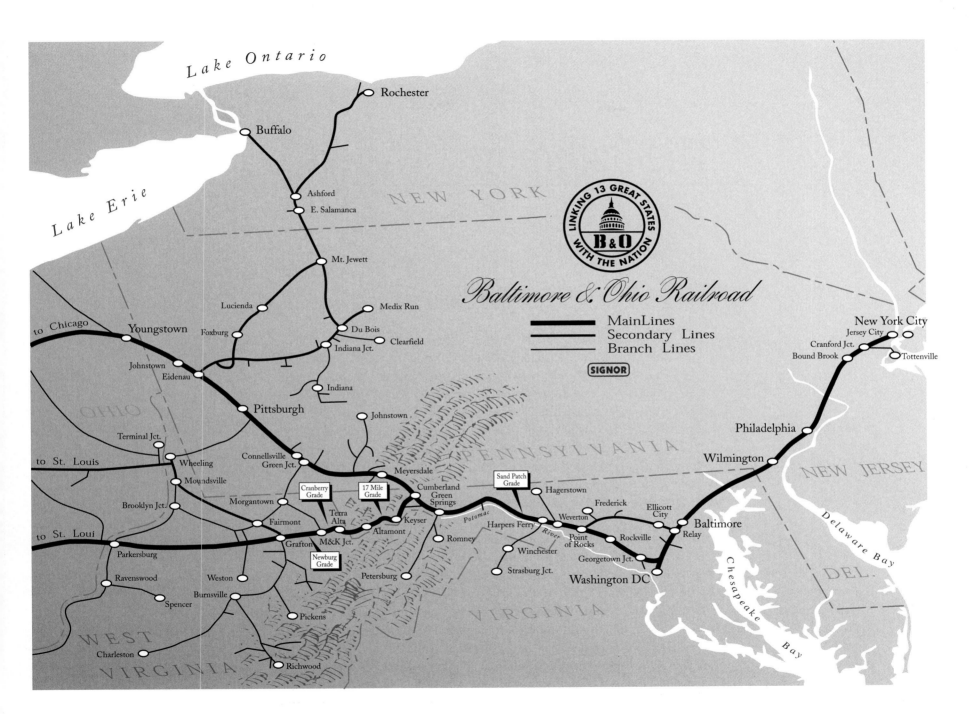

Lake Ontario

Lake Erie

Rochester

Buffalo

NEW YORK

Ashford
E. Salamanca

Mt. Jewett

LINKING 13 GREAT STATES
WITH THE NATION
B&O

Baltimore & Ohio Railroad

MainLines
Secondary Lines
Branch Lines

SIGNOR

New York City
Jersey City
Cranford Jct.
Bound Brook
Tottenville

to Chicago
Lucienda
Medix Run

Youngstown
Foxburg
Du Bois
Clearfield

Johnstown
Eidenau
Indiana Jct.

Philadelphia

to St. Louis
Indiana

Pittsburgh

Wilmington

OHIO

PENNSYLVANIA

NEW JERSEY

Terminal Jct.
Johnstown

Wheeling
Connellsville
Green Jct.
Meyersdale

Moundsville
Cranberry Grade
17 Mile Grade
Cumberland
Green Springs
Sand Patch Grade
Hagerstown

Delaware Bay

Brooklyn Jct.
Morgantown
Terra Alta
Frederick
Ellicott City

to St. Loui
Fairmont
Keyser
Weverton
Baltimore

Parkersburg
Grafton
M&K Jct.
Altamont
Harpers Ferry
Point of Rocks
Rockville
Relay

Ravenswood
Weston
Newburg Grade
Romney
Winchester
Georgetown Jct.

Spencer
Burnsville
Petersburg
Strasburg Jct.

Potomac River

DEL.

Washington DC

Chesapeake Bay

WEST
VIRGINIA
Charleston
Pickens
Richwood

VIRGINIA

11

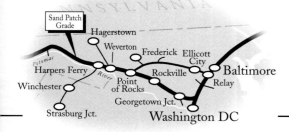

The Baltimore Division

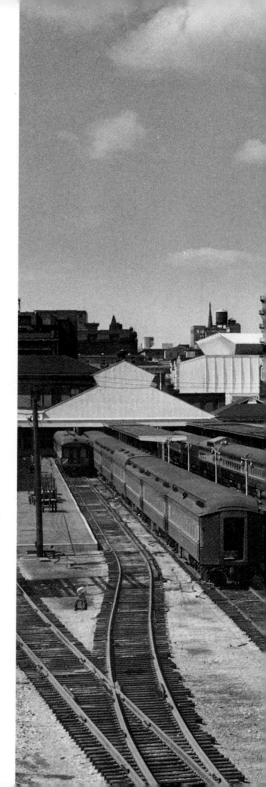

There's no better place to start our photographic visit to the Baltimore & Ohio than its hometown. It was here in 1827 that the railroad got its start when local businessmen, concerned about the loss of commerce to canals into New York, Philadelphia, and Washington, D.C., decided to build a railroad.

Tracks in and around Baltimore were operated as the Baltimore Terminal Division. The Baltimore Division extended from Baltimore as far south as Washington, D.C., and as far west as Weverton, Maryland. Essentially this included the B&O as it existed in the years before and during the Civil War.

In the 1950s the B&O operated more than 130 miles of track in the Terminal Division. Operating a complete marine operation with tugs, carfloats, and dockside connections with oceangoing vessels gave the B&O, and its shippers, a direct connection with the rest of the world. The Baltimore Terminal Division included classification tracks, engine servicing areas, and car and locomotive shops. Within Baltimore it operated two passenger stations: Camden Street and Mount Royal. The company's main headquarters were also located in Baltimore.

The Terminal Division was made up of several subdivisions, including the Sparrows Point Sub, Locust Point Sub, and the Curtis Bay Branch.

With the skyline of Baltimore looming in the background, train no. 5, the *Capitol Limited,* prepares to depart Camden Street Station bound for Washington's Union Station. Camden was the B&O's only station in Baltimore by this time, Mount Royal Station having been closed in 1961. Camden Yards is now the home of the Baltimore Orioles rather than a busy passenger station, but railroading is still the order of the day on this sunny afternoon in May 1963. Photo by J. E. Bradley

The Terminal Division also included the 6.9-mile Baltimore Belt Railroad, the Mount Royal Station trackage, Camden Street Station, and the associated six-building Camden warehouse complex.

Although the Baltimore Terminal Division included numerous yards, interlockings, and switching districts, perhaps none of them are more familiar than the Fells Point area, where extremely tight curves, lots of street trackage, and close clearances made it necessary to employ small locomotives to work the many industrial spurs in the area. The B&O used eight electric locomotives and its famed "Docksider" tank locomotives for this service. In later years, trackmobiles—trucks with couplers— served the Fells Point area until the line was abandoned in 1983.

On to Washington

The Washington Subdivision connected Baltimore with the nation's capital. At Relay, Md., the tracks of the Washington Sub swung away from those of the Old Main Line Sub. Relay's best known railroad landmark is the Thomas Viaduct, a stone-arch bridge that was the largest railroad bridge in the country when completed in 1835. Despite its age, the bridge

continues to serve CSX today, ample evidence of the triumph of overbuilding over time.

In the 1950s the Washington Sub was primarily a passenger railroad, with over 21 scheduled first-class trains in each direction over the double-track line in 1953.

The Washington Sub ended with the connection with the Washington Terminal Railroad at C Tower in Washington, 36 miles from Camden Station. In early years the railroad kept freight trains off the Washington Sub, preferring to keep the line fairly open for passenger travel. In the 1950s three scheduled freight trains each way used the line between Potomac Yard, a large complex just south of Washington in Alexandria, Virginia, and Baltimore. As passenger travel declined, the B&O took freights off the Old Main and used the Washington line, taking advantage of the better speeds possible on the Washington Sub.

Along with the Pennsylvania Railroad; Southern; Richmond, Fredericksburg & Potomac; and Chesapeake & Ohio; the B&O was part owner of the Washington Terminal Railroad, which operated Union Station and its associated passenger and express yards. Freight traffic was handled through

Potomac Yard, one of the first large classification yards built to handle the traffic of more than one railroad. The B&O used the locomotive facilities in Potomac Yard to turn its freight power.

Perhaps the most unusual line was the Georgetown Branch, which meandered through suburban Maryland from Georgetown Junction, just north of Silver Spring, Md., on the Metropolitan Sub heading towards Cumberland, through Bethesda, the short Dalecarlia Tunnel, and into Georgetown proper.

From DC west to Point of Rocks

From Washington west to Weverton, Md., and the connection with the Cumberland Division was known as the Metropolitan Subdivision. This line was completed in the 1860s, when the B&O finished constructing the line between Washington and the existing line at Point of Rocks, Md. Before completion of this 52-mile connection traffic to and from Washington had to be routed via Relay.

This line played host to the *Capitol Limited* and other trains heading into and departing Washington Union Station. Freight traffic consisted primarily of trains between Brunswick, Md., and

Washington. Brunswick was the site of a fairly large classification yard and served as the division point between the Baltimore Division to the east and the Cumberland Division to the west.

Near D.C. the Metropolitan Division served several bedroom communities with scheduled commuter runs. These included Silver Spring, Kensington, Forest Glen, and Rockville. The farther it got from Washington the more rural the Metropolitan Sub looked. By the time it reached Gaithersburg, the scenery consisted of small towns and family farms. At Point of Rocks the junction of the Metropolitan Sub and the Old Main Line Sub was marked by a large brick station, which quickly became a railroad and local landmark.

Old Main Line Subdivision

The aptly named Old Main Line Sub was the original route west from Baltimore through Ellicott City, Sykesville, Mount Airy, Adamstown, and ultimately Point of Rocks. Strangely, the major city of Frederick, Md., was left off the main line and was instead served by a 3.5-mile branch. The Frederick Branch saw regular and frequent passenger service through the end of World War II. Freight service

continued for many years, and successor CSX continues to serve customers in Frederick today.

The original line followed the narrowed, twisting course established by the Patapsco River west until it reached Mount Airy. From there the line followed the Bush Creek until it neared Frederick Junction, where the Frederick Branch connected with the main.

Although an engineering marvel for the 1830s and '40s, the line was outdated by the late 1800s. By the early 1900s the Old Main had been rebuilt. The most noticeable improvement was the completion of a cutoff between Mount Airy and Watersville Junction. This was the most significant portion of a construction project that replaced the 12 worst miles of the Old Main between Monrovia and Woodbine. The rebuilding added seven tunnels to the railroad between Relay and Point of Rocks, including the ½-mile-long Mount Airy Tunnel. When finished, the eastbound grade had been reduced to .9 percent and many of the worst curves had been flattened out.

By the 1940s the Old Main Line had been double-tracked. Train movements were controlled by manned interlocking towers located at strategic points along the line.

Passenger service was removed by the 1940s, with all passenger trains using the Metropolitan Sub to and from Washington.

The Old Main was abandoned east of Mount Airy following damage from Hurricane Agnes in 1972. But in 1974 a resurgence of coal traffic, especially coal bound for ships in Baltimore, meant that the Old Main was rebuilt and reopened. Although primarily a route for coal trains, regular manifest freights also operated over the Old Main as traffic and conditions dictated. Brunswick became a base for helper operations to shove long trains of coal up the .9 percent grade through Mount Airy Tunnel. Ironically, the same line that served the B&O in its infant years was still used for its intended purpose—getting export freight over the mountains to ships in Baltimore—when the railroad was no longer an independent corporate entity.

West from Point of Rocks

Westward from Point of Rocks the line was operated as the Metropolitan Sub as far as Weverton, Md. The operational hub of this stretch of line through the 1950s was Brunswick, Md. Brunswick performed several key roles in the B&O's operations in the region.

The quintessential image of the Baltimore & Ohio in its hometown. The B&O's unique "Docksider" switchers are well known among generations of model railroaders who have enjoyed models of these engines in several scales. The real Docksiders were ideally suited for working short cuts of cars through harrowing curves and tight clearances in and around the industrial cities of the east. Here no. 98 works the night shift, picking up an empty car from the Hearst newspaper warehouse in Baltimore, Md. B&O Railroad Photo

Until 1960, when the Cumberland Yard was expanded, westbound traffic was all blocked into trains at Brunswick.

These trains, essentially long transfer jobs, were run between Brunswick and Bayview, Curtis Bay, and Locust Point (all in Baltimore), and Eckington and Potomac Yards (both in Washington). The eastbounds carried numbers 94 or 96, prefixed by the yard name (for example, Locust Point 94). Westbound trains, all numbered 97, arrived from the three Baltimore yards, Potomac Yard, and Philadelphia and Jersey City. They were then resorted into trains at Brunswick for forwarding to Chicago, Cincinnati, St. Louis, Cleveland, and Pittsburgh—for a total of five hot freights, all numbered "97," leaving Brunswick in the early afternoon.

By the end of the 1950s it was clear Brunswick was unable to handle the traffic demands. The freight reclassification was then shifted farther west to Cumberland.

After the 1960 expansion of the yard facilities in Cumberland, Brunswick lost much of its importance, although the roundhouse and a small yard, primarily for locals to and from Washington, Frederick, and Relay, remained in service well into the diesel era.

Shenandoah Subdivision

The last portion of the Baltimore Division we'll look at is the Shenandoah Sub, which ran from the connection just inside the west portal of the Harpers Ferry Tunnel, 50.4 miles south into Strasburg Junction, Va. There the line connected with the Southern Railway.

The most important town on the line was Winchester, Va., where the B&O interchanged with the Winchester & Western. The W&W served a large sand-loading facility and other local customers, giving those cars to the B&O.

The other major industry on this branch was limestone. Numerous small limestone loading points as far south as Strasburg Junction, and three major ones, were all located in and around Millville, Va.

Although this line never saw much passenger traffic, the B&O did run occasional horse-race specials to the racetracks in Charlestown, West Virginia, as late as the 1960s.

The Shenandoah Division was small-town Southern railroading in Virginia and West Virginia, an interesting contrast to the mainline coal-hauling railroad more familiar to railfans.

The long voyage to the open sea through the Chesapeake Bay is made worthwhile by the well-protected and deep harbor of Baltimore, still one of the finest natural harbors in the United States. That fact was not lost on the early proponents of the B&O, and the connection with shipping remains a critical factor in the city's economy. Here the steamship *Seafair* is riding high alongside Locust Point. Yet another freighter is moored to the same pier in the distance. Tracks run right up to the waterfront. Photo by H. A. McBride, Nov. 1951

▲ Like many railroads B&O sought to utilize Geeps in both passenger and freight service. The so-called "torpedo boat" Geeps, like nos. 746 and 741, seen here accelerating a train out of Camden Street Station, had the air tanks (which some thought looked like shipboard torpedo tubes) atop the long hood to make room for additional water storage capacity between the trucks. The train is no. 119, bound for D.C. Photo by H. N. Proctor, Sept. 25, 1954

▶ The locomotive of an extra train was required to display white flags during the day with white illuminated "class" lights at night, a clear indication to other trains that the extra was not listed in the railroad's timetable. Here the fireman hangs out the white flags on EM-1 2-8-8-4 no. 7609. The class lights are the small lights on both sides of the smokebox. Photo by Jim Shaughnessy

▲ White flags hung and white markers lit, 7609 is ready for her next assignment as an extra. The tender of one of her sisters sits on the arrival track. This is a moody, nighttime look at the B&O in steam. Photo by Jim Shaughnessy

▶ Riverside Yard in Baltimore was the location of a major locomotive servicing facility. A set of F7s takes on fuel in November 1953. Photo by James P. Gallagher

▶▶ There's an eerie stillness in this photo of two diesels — one EMD and one Alco — resting for the night in Riverside Yard in Baltimore, Md. Photo by James P. Gallagher, July 1955

▲ For many years Baltimore was served by its hometown railroad through two stations—Mount Royal and Camden. Here Pacific 5116 leaves the trainshed at Camden Station bound for the nation's capital. The electric line to the left is the Baltimore & Annapolis. Interurban no. 97 is will pace the steamer for a short distance, then swing east towards Annapolis. Photo by Herbert Harwood, 1947

▶ The passengers are all aboard as the conductor gives the engineer the "highball," the signal to proceed. This scene was once repeated thousands of times in towns and cities across the continent. In this case the train is the eastbound Marylander, readying to leave Mount Royal Station in Baltimore, Md. Photo by James P. Gallagher, October 1956.

The approach to Mount Royal Station looks like the invention of a space-starved model railroader. Exiting the "tunnel" formed by the North Avenue stone bridge, the Belt line proper and several secondary tracks crossed the Pennsy's line heading for the Bolton Yard. The tower is the classic standard B&O design. B&O Railroad photo, 1942

▶ In late 1956 a number of Rail Diesel Cars appeared on the roster. Here three of the new cars, in their first revenue run, are pulling into Mount Royal Station in Baltimore, Md. Tracks below are the Pennsylvania Railroad. The Baltimore engine terminal of the Maryland & Pennsylvania Railroad, the famed "Ma & Pa," is just out of the picture to the left, alongside the Pennsy yard. Photo by James Pelham, October 28, 1956

▶▶ The fireman leans way out of the cab, straining to get a better view of the track ahead, as no. 4615 drifts southward over the Pennsy's electrified coachyards with a string of empties. The Mike will soon head through the tunnel and into Mount Royal Station. Photo by John Elder, Jr., May 30, 1951

Number 201, a SW1 built in August 1940, idles as sister no. 200 works a cut of passenger cars in Baltimore, Md. Meanwhile, a crew unloads a gondola spotted on the team track. Note the light-colored (silver) roof on the RPO. Also, note the number of workmen visible in this photo. Railroading in the golden years was indeed a labor-intensive occupation. B&O Railroad Photo, 1944.

A diesel switcher, SW1 no. 203, works a string of cars in Lower Camden Yard near Austin Street in Baltimore, Md. The rods in the foreground are used to throw switches from control towers located alongside the right-of-way. B&O Railroad photo, 1944

▶ The Thomas Viaduct in Relay, Md., provided an ideal setting for many shots of B&O trains over the years. The arched stonework and graceful curve accented the look of many of the road's premier passenger trains. Here the *Washingtonian* strikes a sunlit pose. Number 86, one of seven passenger F3s on the roster, does the honors. Photo by James P. Gallagher, May 1954

▶▶ A commuter local headed by engine no. 1411, an E6, just out of Elk Ridge, Md., and bound for its next stop in St. Denis, about .7 mile distant, heads across the ancient Thomas Viaduct at Relay, Md. Did the original designers of these stone-arch bridges know the size the trains would become one hundred years hence? Most of the stone spans built in the 19th century were abandoned in later years for lack of traffic, not because they couldn't support the weight of modern trains. Photo by James P. Gallagher, May 1951

◄◄ There's little chance of mistaking the setting of this shot. Union Station's location, a mere two blocks north of the Capitol dome, serves as a fitting reminder to the importance the government once placed on rail travel. Once upon a time senators, congressmen, and presidents, generals and admirals, and visiting foreign dignitaries got their first, and often their last, look at the nation's capital from a viewpoint similar to this one. Where once hundreds of trains from five railroads (B&O, C&O, Southern, Pennsylvania, Richmond, Fredericksburg & Potomac) used this station, today only Amtrak and commuter trains call here. The station proper has been lovingly restored. Photo by A. D. Hooks, May 31, 1947

◄ Potomac Yard, located in Alexandria, Va., just south of Washington, D.C. A B&O F unit has arrived with a southbound train, while a trio of Pennsy GG1 electrics await their next assignment. Photo by J. P. Lamb, September 1961

◀◀ Looks as if the railfans are coming up out of the weeds! Number 4320 pops out of the Dalecarlia Tunnel on the Georgetown branch just over the Washington D.C.—Maryland border with a railfan trip in tow. Photo by Howard Davis, June 1948

◀ Not everyone is enthusiastic about the arrival of E8 no. 95 at the handsome brick station in Silver Spring, Md. The classic lineup of General Motors (and others) products was located along the line to D.C. Silver Spring is the first stop out of the nation's capital for many trains. B&O Railroad photo

The *Diplomat* races northbound for Baltimore out of Washington behind another clean set of gray and blue E units. The previous day's light dusting of snow won't affect the schedule. The train has just passed through Relay, Md., visible between the barren trees in the background. James P. Gallagher photo, February 1955

A tip of the hat, a timeless pose as a young man pauses from riding his trusty steed to salute a much faster speed demon. Large numbers on the front of diesel locomotives were easier for lineside tower operators to read. Reflective patterns made them stand out, even at night or in low visibility. Photo by James P. Gallagher, November 4, 1953

This diesel-powered freight is on the "Old Main" at Ilchester, Md., bound for Brunswick. The train is crossing the Patapsco River on a double-track truss bridge. Continuing its journey west to Point of Rocks, the train will run parallel to the Patapsco, taking advantage of the relatively easy grades on the south bank of the river to work its way through the mountains. Photo by James P. Gallagher, August 1952

The B&O's T-3b class 4-8-2s, such as no. 5572, were quite handsome machines. The boilers were relatively clean of exterior plumbing and other fittings, giving them a lean, racy look ideally suited for passenger service. Some of the T3s were painted blue to match the railroad's passenger equipment. Number 5572 is easing onto the turntable at Brunswick, Md. Brunswick was where westbound trains were reclassified until those functions were moved to Cumberland by the end of the steam era. Photo by James P. Gallagher, October 1952

▶ The railroad imposed a 10 mph speed limit over the Potomac River bridge, making it easy for photographers to get a good shot. Mallet 7625, an EM-1 class 2-8-8-4, drifts across the river on October 5, 1952. The engine will take this train as far east as Brunswick, Md., the easternmost point the Mallets served by this date. Photo by James P. Gallagher

▶▶ Harpers Ferry, W.Va., was located at the confluence of the Potomac and Shenandoah Rivers. The western terminus of the B&O during the railroad's early years, it was the scene of abolitionist John Brown's failed attempt to encourage a slave uprising. Harpers Ferry also hosted one of the most elaborate train robberies in history during the Civil War, when Stonewall Jackson captured 56 locomotives and 300 cars from the railroad, transporting them to the south. Almost a century later a set of handsome E units leads an eastbound passenger job across the Potomac River bridge. Photo by James P. Gallagher, 1958.

▶ Many railroads, including the B&O, assigned one number to multiunit diesel lashups when they were first delivered. Therefore the A-B-B-A set of FTs pulling Train 97 through Harpers Ferry is locomotive no. 5. Problems crept up when one unit of a multiunit set needed maintenance, meaning other locomotives would have to be taken off line. The diesels shown here took the train in Philadelphia and will handle the 106 cars all the way to Willard, Ohio. Train 97 offered 51-hour scheduled freight service between New York and Chicago. Photo by E. L. Thompson

▶▶ Wagontop caboose 2800 brings up the markers and is about to dive into Harpers Ferry Tunnel. The exposed rockwork on the near-vertical cliff face lends a sense of drama to the scenery. The curved station platform is visible on both sides of track, as is the other end of this fairly short bore built in 1896 and rebuilt in 1931. Photo by Gerald Brimacombe, October 1963

◄◄ In 1949 the B&O introduced two new trains, named *Columbians.* These were the first trains in the east equipped with dome cars, a type of dome called a Strata-dome, with a lower profile so the car could operate in the lower clearances typically found on eastern railroads. In addition to new equipment, the train was also intended to offer roomy accommodations and top-notch service, all for regular coach fares, in the D.C.-to-Chicago route. The train is posed for its official portrait on the Carollton Viaduct.

◄ Although they're mostly gone or boarded up today, interlocking towers once played a critical role in getting trains over the line. Most towers were two-story with banks of large windows on two sides and in front, affording a fairly un-obstructed view of the main line. The view from HX Tower in Halethorpe, Md., can be seen here as train no. 18, the *Cleveland Night Express,* heads eastbound with two Geeps and five cars. The train was a Cleveland-to-Baltimore run via Washington, D.C. Photo by H. N. Proctor, October 31, 1954

◀◀ The *Cincinnatian,* the railroad's "other" streamlined steamer (the first was the *Royal Blue*), heads west on its last run between Baltimore and Cincinnati. Headed by President-class 4-6-2 no. 5301, the train is ripping through the resort town of Mountain Lake Park, Md., greeted only by another photographer, also on hand to capture this obscure, but historic, moment. Photo by William Price, June 24, 1950

◀ The pride evident in this shot goes far beyond the glistening coat on F7 no. 281, leading train no. 87 west to Washington. Note the well-maintained track, complete absence of litter, and the razor-sharp ballast line separating the gravel ballast from the darker cinder fill. That's Fort Meade Junction, Md., in the background. The track at the right leads to the passing track, wye, and the 4.2-mile branch known as the Fort George G. Meade Subdivision. Photo by H. N. Proctor, August 16, 1953.

West to Cumberland

FT set no. 5 teams up with an S-1 on a manifest freight through North Branch, Md., located south of Cumberland on the main line approximately 2 miles west of Patterson Creek. The train will soon arrive at the junction of the Patterson Cutoff and the main line. Note the automobile getting some needed attention in the distance, and the crisply maintained track-work. Photo by Wayne Brumbaugh

From Weverton, Maryland, the B&O main line continued west as the Cumberland Division. Proceeding west through the Maryland countryside the line worked its way through historic Harpers Ferry, then ran along the winding banks of the Potomac River valley through Cherry Run and on to Hancock, the site of a broad sweeping curve favored by photographers over the years, and the location of a junction with the branch to Berkeley Springs.

The line then turned southwest, still following the natural path the river cut through the mountains, reaching Magnolia, the location of the Magnolia Cutoff, another construction project dating to the early years of the 20th century to reduce grades faced by eastbound trains. Through this entire area the Western Maryland main line between Hagerstown and Cumberland was on the opposite bank of the Potomac. At Patterson Creek the line split, with one line heading west towards McKenzie, West Virginia, and the other heading into Cumberland proper.

Cumberland was the so-called Queen City of the Alleghenies. Located 175 miles west of Baltimore, Cumberland was the initial goal of the B&O. Arriving in the city in 1842, the B&O immediately became an integral part of the city's life. It was here that three of the railroad's most important and historic lines converged: the main line from Baltimore, the so-called West

End line, which went to Grafton, W.Va., and ultimately St. Louis, and the Pittsburgh Division line to Pittsburgh and Chicago. Cumberland itself is in a narrow, deep valley formed by the North Branch of the Potomac River. A second railroad, the Western Maryland, also had a significant presence in Cumberland.

The centerpiece of the B&O in Cumberland was the Queen City Hotel, a railroad-owned hotel that also served as the B&O's passenger station. All trains, both freight and passenger, changed crews and locomotives here, the only exception being the trains that used the Patterson Creek Cutoff to bypass the city entirely.

As one would expect of a major division point, Cumberland boasted a complex of locomotive-servicing and repair facilities. While the railroad always maintained a yard here, after World War II more yard capacity was added as Cumberland replaced Brunswick as the major westbound reclassification facility for traffic in and out of Baltimore and points east. While the eastbound yard just east of Virginia Avenue was left relatively intact, a new yard for westbound classification was built across the main line.

Perhaps one of the most interesting railroad facilities at Cumberland was the Cumberland Rolling Mill, an early recycling operation owned and operated by the B&O. Scrap metal of all types was hauled in from throughout the entire railroad, melted down, and re-rolled for use in new cars, bridges, and rail. In addition to the railroad facilities, Cumberland also played host to several major railroad customers including Kelly-Springfield Tires and the Queen City Brewing Co., makers of Queen City beer.

At Viaduct Junction the Pittsburgh Division line continued along the banks of Wills Creek, while the line to St. Louis swung away and crossed the creek at a right angle on its way to Grafton. Adding to the maze of trackage in this area was the Western Maryland line to Connellsville, located slightly below the B&O in most places as it headed towards its station on Mechanic Street, a few blocks south of the Queen City station. The WM would parallel the B&O through the famed Cumberland Narrows as far as Connellsville, Pennsylvania.

Williams Street Yard, yet another of the many yards in Cumberland, was used for interchange with the WM. On the north end of this yard was the WM station—the WM's own Ridgeley Yard was south of the station across the Potomac in West Virginia. For several miles south of the city the WM line to Elkins and the B&O West End line towards St. Louis ran on opposite banks of the river.

The Queen City Hotel served for many years as the B&O's station in Cumberland until it fell to the wrecker's ball in 1972. But those days are in the future as brand-new E7 no. 70 sits in front of the Cumberland, Md., station in 1946. No. 70 and her 18 sisters will soon render the over-track water spout, built to water Pacifics and Mountains, superfluous. Photo by Louis Marre

The Cumberland, Md., station is unmistakable. Here 4-8-2 no. 5051 readies to leave on the point of a passenger train. The Mountain will serve as a road engine for a double-headed climb through the narrows and up Sand Patch (note helper coupled to 4-8-2s tender). Photo by Phillip E. Thomas, Harold K. Vollrath Collection, June 1945

◀◀ A Big Six, no. 6144, works hard eastbound near Hancock, Md., with a long string of twin bay hoppers heaped high with black diamonds. Note the well-maintained multitrack line. B&O Railroad photo

◀ McKenzie Tower, "CO" in railroad parlance, guarded the junction between the western end of the Patterson Creek Cutoff and the main line. The train is coming off the main line from Cumberland, heading west. About a mile east of the junction the Cutoff dives into Knobley Tunnel. Photo by William Price, October 13, 1949

▶ An A-B-B-A set of FTs, led by no. 5, uses its combined 5,400 h.p. to lead a long freight just west of Hancock, Md. The diesels proved their worth in helper service on the West End but by the summer of 1946 diesels were also quickly replacing EM-1s and S-1as in time freight service. B&O Railroad photo

▶▶ Although Baltimore & Ohio was an EMD stronghold, the railroad also sampled first-generation diesel power from other builders such as Alco. Here an A-B-A set of FA-2s assists an EM-1 westbound on the Cumberland Division near Patterson Creek, Md. Photo by William Price, April 5, 1951

◄◄ A key feature of the "High Line" between Brunswick and Cumberland, Md., was Carothers Tunnel. Here Big Six 2-10-2 no. 6209 bursts forth from the west portal bound for Cumberland with time freight 97 in tow. Photo by Bruce D. Fales, October 1946

◄ The craggy rock outcropping looming over the Cumberland Narrows is barely visible through the smoke hanging over Cumberland roundhouse. An impressive array of B&O steam power, including a number of 2-10-2s, 2-8-8-0s, and 0-8-8-0s sits idle on the outside storage tracks. Surplus power was the result of a strike in the soft coal mines in April 1934. Photo by Bruce Fales, April 8, 1934

▲ It must be mighty warm in the cab of S-1a class 6113 as she assists a pair of Geeps out of Cumberland in July 1955. Note the crossing guard and the switch frog located in the street. Two more S-1as will be added to the train in Hyndman. Photo by Robert M. Pringle, July 1955

▶ Many railroads, including the B&O, tried Rail Diesel Cars (RDCs), essentially self-contained passenger trains, as a way to make money or at least curtail losses on marginal passenger runs. Here a trio of RDCs on a special run are stopped in the front of the Cumberland, Md., station. Note the basic dark green paint scheme on the U.S. Mail truck, a far cry from today's red, white, and blue. B&O Railroad photo, 1955

▶ Train no. 22, the eastbound *Washingtonian,* glides into Cumberland behind a 4-6-2. Pacifics, built for fast passenger service on the eastern lines, found their way into Cumberland Division service as diesels bumped them from their earlier runs. Wayne Brumbaugh photo, 1951

▶▶ Steam locomotives required constant care and attention, both on and off the high line. Number 7609, a mighty EM-1 2-8-8-4, gets a beauty treatment before her next assignment out of Cumberland, Md. The Cumberland facility included both covered and open stall tracks. Photo by Gene Donaldson

◀ This shot provides a good look at the consist in the eastbound *Cincinnatian,* train no. 76, as it passes McKenzie Tower. Using the Patterson Creek Cutoff trimmed 10 miles off the train's run between Cincinnati and Washington, D.C., although it meant bypassing Cumberland. Photo by William P. Price, April 26, 1947

▲ The conductor and engineer of no. 7101 cool their heels awaiting E7 no. 70 with a special passenger job at McKenzie Interlocking. The interlocking guarded the junction between the line to Cumberland and the Patterson Creek Cutoff. The freight is heading out from Cumberland; the passenger train is coming off the Cutoff, having bypassed the Queen City. Photo by William P. Price, May 30, 1947

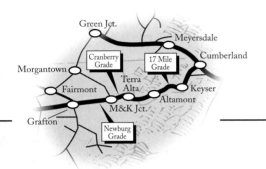

West from Cumberland to Coal Country

Altamont, W.Va., on the West End was the summit of the Alleghenies and one of the highest points with main line rails in the eastern U.S. Here a trio of F7s have crested the summit and are ready to begin their trip downhill with a long string of hoppers in tow. David P. Morgan Library Collection

Generalizations are, of course, dangerous. It's very easy to generalize that a railroad was a passenger road, a bridge route, or a granger road. But sometimes generalizations do hold true. To many people the Baltimore & Ohio is first and foremost a coal-hauling railroad. While the B&O was certainly more than that, there's no denying the importance of coal traffic to the railroad's bottom line.

In 1940 U.S. soft coal production measured 461 million tons, 36 million of which were carried by the B&O. In 1958 coal was still a single-commodity king on the B&O; the railroad hauled over 11 percent of the national production. This good news was dampened somewhat by the fact that coal consumption was down as railroads, including the B&O, looked to diesel locomotives and as oil and gas replaced coal as a commercial heating source. This national trend toward lowered coal consumption wasn't reversed until the oil crisis of the early 1970s. But if you stood trackside by the Baltimore & Ohio, it would be difficult to imagine this railroad was anything but a coal-hauler.

Of course, you'd have to be in the right place, and to catch B&O coal-hauling action there was no other place more "right" than the line between Cumberland, Maryland, and Grafton, West Virginia.

Essentially the western half of the Cumberland Division, the line climbed through some of the most rugged and beautiful country in the eastern U.S. It presented a challenge to builders and train crews equal to that found anywhere.

Three or more fire-breathing steel monsters, often one or more on the head end with two or more behind, spliced by 100+ carloads of West Virginia coal wound through the Appalachian valleys every day. Breaking up the potential monotony of solid strings of hoppers was an assortment of mixed freights. While hardly a passenger thoroughfare, the West End played host to two name passenger trains, the *National Limited* and the *Diplomat*.

◄◄ Two Baltimore & Ohio signature items are visible here. The 7133 is one of 30 EL-3 class 2-8-8-0s on the roster. Note the dual front headlights above the pilot deck. Instantly recognizable as B&O is the wagontop caboose. The caboose has just emerged from the double-track eastbound Kingwood Tunnel. The steamers are about to enter the single-track westbound tunnel. William Price photo, April 30, 1948.

◄ A set of three F3s and a Big Six no. 6105 combine horsepower to assist a loaded coal drag toward the summit of the Allegheny Mountains in Garrett, Pennsylvania. The train is snaking its way along the Casselman River. A pair of GP9s is pulling out of sight, on the head end. Photo by Philip R. Hastings

▶ A B&O "Timesaver" freight barrels eastbound toward Cumberland as it runs along the Potomac River through Piedmont, W.Va. Just visible across the river to the right is the part of the enormous West Virginia Pulp & Paper Co. complex. Photo by James P. Gallagher, July 1957

▶▶ This photo illustrates the changing of the guard as internal combustion power made inroads on the dominance of the steam locomotive during and after World War II. One of the B&O's most modern steamers, EM-1 class 2-8-8-4 no. 7606, is in charge of a heavy coal drag entering the yard limits at West Keyser. On the main line carded time freight 94 behind "diesel unit no. 7," a set of FTs, overtakes the steamer — a symbolic portrait. Photo by H. W. Pontin, June 1945

▶ R Tower is visible just ahead of the trio of F units leading a train of empties that will shortly crawl up the Cheat River grade. The engine house serves as a base for helpers. The large machine shop addition (to the left of the engine house, just behind the fuel tanks) and the tanks themselves were added when diesel helpers arrived at M&K Junction in the late 1940s. Photo by Frank E. Shaffer, 1960

▶▶ Diesels, like F7 no. 186, quickly superseded steam in helper service out of M&K Junction. Some steamers, like the one in the distance, could still be found around the engine house awaiting a call to service. The green flags on the diesels indicate that they are being readied for a second section.

▲ Number 7613 was a fairly new EM-1 class 2-8-8-4 when she was handling this assignment—another long coal train through Amblersburg, W.Va., on Cranberry Grade, heading east toward Terra Alta. Photo by H. W. Pontin

▲ right: Amblersburg, W.Va., featured a sweeping curve that was a favorite haunt for railfans bent on catching the coal action. The lead Mallet has a bone in her teeth leading yet another seemingly endless string of hoppers. Here we see them after they cut off from the train. Photo by Charles A. Brown, March 20, 1948

▶ As those hoppers passed, the photographer turned to his left and caught this view of two more Mallets pushing hard on the rear of the train. Note the various grades of coal and the differences between the individual hopper cars. Photo by Charles A. Brown, March 20, 1948

◀ The two pushers are closing in, still shoving on the bay window hack. Baltimore & Ohio was unique among railroads in its preference for wagontop-designed cars such as this caboose. Thousands of boxcars and covered hoppers were built using the same basic design. The "wagontop" name comes from the similarity between the cars and the early Conestoga wagons, many of which started their long journey westward on the National Road, which carved a route through the same territory as the B&O. Photo by Charles A. Brown, March 20, 1948

▲ Every spot on a railroad has a name, from the largest granite terminal to the simplest siding. Their work done, the two helpers have cut off the back of the train and are drifting back downgrade past the small shack, which wears a sign identifying it as "Amblersburg" to all concerned. The shack would be gone by 1950, the steamers would last a few years longer. But those days are still in the future and the helpers will be back shoving hard on the tail of another drag before too long. Photo by Charles A. Brown, March 20, 1948

◀ Diesels were quick to prove their worth in pusher service. Multiunit diesels eliminated the second crew needed for two steam helpers. Fuel and maintenance costs were also lower. And, according to some reports, the diesels shortened the climb up Cranberry Grade by 35 minutes over steam-powered trains. Here A-B set of F7s no. 192 and a second unidentified set swing onto Salt Lick Curve into the summit of the climb at Terra Alta, W.Va. Photo by H. W. Pontin

▲ The photographer's position and angle emphasize the vertical curve in the track in this shot near Terra Alta, W.Va. Photo by Charles Brown, October 21, 1945.

Number 7170, last of the EL-5a class 2-8-8-0s, is climbing Newburg Grade near Austen, W.Va., with a 54-car coal drag. Two more 2-8-8-0s are shoving on the rear. These 58-inch-drivered locomotives were ideal for work on the mountainous West End beyond Cumberland. Like all but two of her sisters (7163 and 7148), 7170 was simplified in the late 1920s, a move that boosted each locomotive's tractive effort to 118,800 pounds. The large 18,000-gallon tender was another modification that improved performance. Photo by R. H. Kindig, July 1949

Without the dramatic smoke and steam of the uphill trains, this 50-car westbound extra seems as if it's sitting still. But EM-1 no. 7614 is definitely moving. The 2-8-8-4 is heading down Cranberry Grade just below Terra Alta, W.Va. Photo by R. H. Kindig, July 1949

Coupled to the rear of a bay-window caboose — not a wagontop this time — two helpers, class LL-1 0-8-8-0 nos. 7047 and 7049, top the grade eastbound into Terra Alta. Photo by Bert Pennypacker, June 29, 1947

Terra Alta again. Same day, different train (note caboose). As the eastbound tops the grade, the two pushers open up wide to bunch the train, the pin is pulled, and the pushers cut off on the fly. Brakes on the helpers are thrown into emergency so they won't ram the rear of the freight train if it suddenly halts (an unlikely event). Photo by Bert Pennypacker, June 29, 1947

Mountain railroading is a constant series of curves and hills. Locating engineers fought tooth and nail to avoid expensive tunnels. But such savings were a trade-off: What the railroad saved up front in construction costs it would ultimately pay for in operating costs. But mountain railroading produced unforgettable images such as this. It's a good thing they couldn't tunnel under all the mountains. Photo by Charles A. Brown

▶ These two Q-4 class Mikados assisted the eastbound *Diplomat* into Terra Alta, W.Va. Before cutting off the train during this unscheduled stop, the Mike on the right will be turned on the wye, while the one on the left will continue on to Keyser, W.Va., with the train. Photo by Bert Pennypacker

▶ below: Although the Mallets were assigned to tackle the heavy coal and manifest trains up Cranberry Grade, the local freights and passenger jobs drew smaller power. Mikado no. 4423, one of 46 Q-4 class 2-8-2s built in 1921, steps westbound out of Terra Alta with a local freight in tow. Photo by Bert Pennypacker

▶▶ Two Mallets, EL-5a no. 7153 and EL-3a 7133, team up behind one of the railroad's unique "wagontop" cabooses to shove a long coal train up Newburg Hill. One hundred cars ahead, no. 7170 strains at the head end. Photo by Dick Kindig, Summer 1950

▶ EM-1 no. 7603 nears the summit of the climb up Cranberry Grade. The 2-8-8-4 was used as an exhibition locomotive at the Chicago Railroad Fair in 1948. Here she's shown in early 1951, hard at work in the service she was designed and built for. Photo by H. W. Pontin

▶▶ The 30 EM-1s, built in 1944-45, were the last steam locomotives built for the Baltimore & Ohio. They're also considered to be the finest steamers ever built for the railroad. Here 7605 is on her maiden voyage up Cranberry Grade, cresting the hill in Terra Alta, W.Va., in 1945. Modelers will appreciate this view of the top of this massive 2-8-8-4. Photo by H. W. Pontin

◄◄ A pair of 2-8-8-0s, class EL-1 no. 7108 and class EL-3 no. 7133, put on a tremendous show of smoke, sand, and steam, as they tackle gravity to boost a coal train up Newburg Grade through Austen, W.Va. This was what late steam-era railroading on the West End was all about. With the coming of diesels the climb remained just as steep but was certainly much less dramatic. Photo by Bruce Fales, August 1950

◄ Streamlined P-7d no. 5301 leads the *Cincinnatian* westbound up the 2.08 percent Cheat River grade. The train is crossing the Tray Run Viaduct on the West End of the Cumberland Division. The photographer notes that the five-car train was making about 15 mph. Photo by Bruce Fales, August 1949

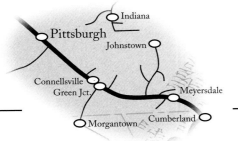

Through the Narrows to Pittsburgh

T he Pittsburgh Division originated at Viaduct Junction, located within the city limits just west of the Queen City Hotel. North of the city the track found a natural routing toward Connellsville, Pennsylvania. This gap, actually the valley for Wills Creek, is known as the "Cumberland Narrows."

The B&O worked its way along the east bank of the creek, while the Western Maryland used the west bank. The looming mountains, with a unique series of rock outcroppings forming an ideal backdrop, made the Narrows an irresistible spot for photographers over the years.

The most challenging stretch of track on the Pittsburgh Division, and one of the most famed grades in the eastern United States, was called Sand Patch. It started at Q Tower in Hyndman, Pa., where an engine house and coaling pocket were located for the helper locomotives. "Helper" on Sand Patch through the late steam era meant S and S-1a class 2-10-2s. While some of the mighty EM-1s spent their twilight years on Sand Patch, the 2-10-2s, the railroad's so-called "Big Sixes," were the main show.

Most westbound freights required a set of helpers, typically two of the class S-1a 2-10-2s. While occasionally helpers were coupled onto trains in Cumberland, helpers

were still busy at Hyndman.

Sand Patch, like many railroad grades, is not an even steady climb. Out of Hyndman it was a slight 1.5 percent. As trains ran farther up the hill, the grade got steeper, topping off at 1.95 percent just beyond Mance Tower. The summit of the climb is just beyond the west portal of Sand Patch Tunnel. The helpers were usually cut off the train just short of the east portal, since the bulk of the train would have been beyond the west portal and therefore over the crest of the hill.

Once off the hill, trains rounded the sweeping curve at Mance, another spot favored by photographers over the years. The line then dropped down a steady one percent

By the time this photo was taken in late 1948, the FTs had been renumbered with a "10" in front of their original road numbers. Here FT no. 105 pulls a freight through the Narrows outside of Cumberland, Maryland. Photo by Robert Chase

With its characteristic off-center bell clearly visible on the front of the smokebox, Big Six 6145 leads a merchandise job southbound out of Mount Savage Junction, three miles north of Cumberland on the Pittsburgh Division. Photo by William P. Price, August 21, 1949

grade through Meyersdale and Salisbury, two locations where the B&O passed beneath the main line of the Western Maryland.

Although most eastbound trains made it up the one percent grade without an assist, there was a helper pocket in Garrett in case an eastbound needed a shove. Eastbound helpers would often run all the way up through Sand Patch Tunnel.

Once in Salisbury the Pittsburgh Division started to follow an easy water-level course along the Youghiogheny River. In Connellsville the B&O interchanged with the Pennsylvania Railroad and the Pittsburgh & Lake Erie. Between McKeesport through Pittsburgh and on to Newcastle most B&O trains used the P&LE, as that line provided an easier route than the B&O's own rails.

As it was on the main line to Pittsburgh, and ultimately Chicago, the Pittsburgh Division was an important link in the B&O system. Heavy traffic, helper operations, and some of the most spectacular scenery in the East made it a great place to watch and photograph trains in the classic era. Here's a brief look at this fascinating stretch of railroad.

▲ A westbound freight leans into the superelevated curve in the Narrows just outside Cumberland, Md. Modelers will note the interesting assortment of freight cars coupled to the drawbar of the Big Six in this train. Robert Collin photo, 1949

▶ This photo provides a wonderful view of Cumberland Narrows. Two railroads, a road, and a river all share the winding natural passage through the Appalachians. The tracks on the right are B&O leased from the Cumberland and Pennsylvania; across the river and roadway is the main line of the Western Maryland, heading for Connellsville, Pa. The single-track line crossing the B&O in the distance is the WM's State Line branch, which connected with the Pennsylvania Railroad in State Line, Pa. The photographer is looking down from Lover's Leap as a B&O 2-10-2 leads a freight through the Narrows. Photo by James P. Gallagher, September 30, 1953

▶ Number 5662 is usually assigned to the Newark Division in Ohio, but she'll have to earn her keep all the way home. The Mountain, built for passenger service, has just finished an overhaul in the Cumberland Back Shops. Before returning home she's leading a train of limestone and merchandise through the sweeping curve through Mance, Pa. A pair of 2-10-2s, the 6102 and 6148, are shoving on the rear. Photo by William Price, June 23, 1954

▶▶ In the days before UPS and FedEx, railroads provided much of the express service needed to keep business moving. Long trains of express cars, like this westbound descending the grade from Sand Patch in Keystone, Pa., looked like passenger trains, hauled freight (and mail), and ran on passenger schedules. Pacific no. 5086 has the honors. Photo by William Price, April 5, 1947

▶ Although freights usually required helpers on Sand Patch grade, most passenger trains could make the hill with a single class T-3 4-8-2 on the point. The sun highlights the details on the front of no. 5566 as she works train no. 22, the *Washingtonian,* up the hill. Photo by S. K. Bolton, Jr., February, 1953.

▶▶ The 1940s and '50s weren't only decades of tremendous change on the head end, but also in the cars that made up the trains. Wood and composite cars, often built in the teens and twenties, and pressed into service long past original estimates because of the Depression and World War II, finally gave way to steel cars of ever-increasing capacity. Close to a half-century of freight car design is demonstrated in this train, a westbound in Manila, Pa., on the Pittsburgh Division. Oh, yes — those two 2-10-2s shoving on the rear are also quite interesting. Photo by William Price, October 1949

◄◄ Perhaps the only thing more impressive than a steam locomotive heading towards you is the sight of one thundering away. Here not one, but two 2-10-2 pushers work an eastbound freight up Sand Patch. The train is bound for Cumberland, Md. The line dieselized fairly early, but 2-8-8-0s and Big Sixes could be found here until 1955. Photo by S. K. Bolton, Jr., July 1950

◄ Falls Cut Tunnel is another one of those spots that looks like it belongs on a model railroad, not the main line of one of the busiest railroads in the east. One of the 2-10-2s bursts forth from clouds of her own making. She's shoving hard on the wagontop caboose on this westbound freight. Photo by Wayne Brumbaugh, 1950

◀◀ Heading east on the westbound main, GP9 5960 emerges from the east portal of Sand Patch Tunnel. This also marks the summit of the climb up Sand Patch grade. The Geep is hauling a work train. Photo by Bill Rettberg

◀ It's 1956, the last year for steam power on the Pittsburgh Division. Looks like Big Six no. 6222 hasn't gotten the word about her impending retirement. She's pulling mightily along the shores of the Beaver River through Wampum, Pa. This is one of two routes between New Castle and Pittsburgh. One route follows the P&W line through hills, and this one is a water-level route — the tracks belong to the Pittsburgh & Lake Erie. B&O has trackage rights on this stretch of that line. Photo by Stephen Gary, January 1956

There's barely an inch to spare for 125-foot-long EM-1 class no. 7614 on the 115-foot turntable at New Castle, Pa. Several other stalls are occupied on this overcast early spring day in the Alleghenies. Photo by W. H. N. Rossiter, April 17, 1954

◀ Up front a pair of GP9s are pulling this long freight through Rockwood, Pa. The pusher is 6105, one of the railroad's 156 Santa Fe-type 2-10-2s. To crews and fans they're known as Big Sixes, hulking locomotives ideally suited to a variety of assignments up front or shoving on the rear. Photo by Phil Hastings

◄◄ Extra 7608 West, a steel train from Johnstown, Pa., arrives in Green Junction, Pa., just east of Connellsville Yard. That's the Western Maryland track in the distance on the other side of the Youghiogheny River. The beautifully lit EM-1 is smoking it up for the photographer, drifting through the yard but producing copious quantities of photogenic soot. Photo by Phil Hastings, August 1954

◄ A T-3 class 4-8-2, demoted from pulling the varnish, leads a string of empty hoppers into Connellsville, Pa., yard. This is the West End of the famed Sand Patch grade. West of here a single Mountain can handle the chores. For the assault on Sand Patch itself the train will require multiple diesel units. Photo by Jim Shaughnessy

▶ One of the Western Maryland's chunky but undeniably handsome Decapods, no. 1120, waits in the clear for B&O no. 7616 near Williamsport, Md. The photo was not taken on the B&O, since B&O trains used WM rails between Cherry Run and Hagerstown, Md. The WM Decapod will help the B&O train up the hill into Hagerstown Yard. William Price photo, April 17, 1952

▶▶ As steam motive power started disappearing, a new hobby — railfanning — was emerging. The two events coincided wonderfully, producing a wonderful record of railroading in the steam era. Clubs and groups around the country chartered excursion trips, like this one behind EM-1 no. 7600, leaving Herrs Island in Pittsburgh, bound for Fairport Harbor, Ohio. The special was chartered by Pittsburgh Electric Railway Club members, several of whom can be seen here in prime "seats" directly behind the tender. Photo by J. J. Young, Jr., October 1956

▶ A nicely matched set of Alco FAs and FBs leads a time freight headed up by a block of reefers along the Ohio River on P&LE tracks just below the Point in Pittsburgh, Pa. The large building in the background is the United States Steel Supply Division. The barge's cargo may not be as perishable as the trains, but it's just as important to the economy of the Steel City. Photo by Ralph Hallock, May 7, 1955

▶▶ Universally acclaimed as the "diesel that did it," the EMD FT proved its worth time after time, and one by one railroads replaced their steam locomotives with the FT's classic bullnose profile. World War II didn't cause, but certainly accelerated, the change. Baltimore & Ohio's original four-unit set, number 1, clips past with a long freight on the Pittsburgh Division, just a few miles west of Cumberland. Photo by William Price, September 19, 1947

◀ GR Tower marks Manila—one of the stiffest parts of the climb up Sand Patch. Articulated no. 7120, a 2-8-8-0, is working hard, assisted by a pair of 2-10-2s shoving out of sight on the rear end. Part of the train is visible in the distance, just to the left of the tower. Photo by William Price, October 11, 1949

▲ Another Big Six, this time the 6200, smokes up West Newton, Pa. As in many eastern cities, the railroad ran through town on a path of its own that looked almost like an alley. Residential and commercial buildings crowded the right-of-way, creating the impression that the trains were running through brick canyons. Photo by D. R. Connor, November 5, 1946

On to the Big Apple

The *Capitol Limited,* one of B&O's premier passenger trains, leaves Jersey City, N.J., bound for Washington, D.C., and points west. The Manhattan skyline has changed since this photo was taken in the late 1930s, but astute fans of New York architecture will recognize several of the skyscrapers in the distance. The train is being pulled by one of the railroad's famed P class 4-6-2s. Photo by S. K. Caites

As noted in the first chapter, the B&O's New York City access was the result of a chess game played in the late 19th century with the Pennsylvania Railroad. By the late steam era, the B&O had firmly established its access into Philadelphia. From Park Junction, just north of the City of Brotherly Love, it had access to Staten Island via operating agreements with the Central Railroad of New Jersey and the Reading dating back to the 1880s.

The route from Baltimore to Park Junction was part of the Baltimore Division, but it's easier to include that stretch of track in the chapter on operations to and from New York, since the line operated between Baltimore and the Big Apple as a single entity. In other words, few through freight and passenger trains terminated in Philadelphia. Instead, the long-haul trains continued through over the rails of the CNJ and Reading, using B&O power and crews.

The Reading provided close to 60 miles of track between Park Junction, Pennsylvania, and Bound Brook, New Jersey. Trackage rights over the CNJ were between Bound Brook to Jersey City, a distance of 32 miles.

Although the railroad's publicity department loved to herald its access to the lucrative New York market, saying that B&O passenger trains went to New York City is a bit of misnomer. In reality passengers had to get off the train in Jersey City and board a bus, which was then loaded onto a ferry for the final mile or so across the Hudson River into Manhattan.

Freight traffic originated and terminated in the Jersey City yard, although a tug and carfloat operation run by the B&O in conjunction with the CNJ after 1934 served to deliver freight into Manhattan. The B&O's New York lines were among the first to dieselize in the U.S.—rugged boxcab units that continued to soldier on years even after "new" diesel locomotives had been retired.

▶ One of the B&O's 84 Q-4b class 2-8-2s, the 4494, is on the point of a westbound freight bound for Baltimore through Aberdeen, Maryland. The second locomotive is one of the railroad's 46 Q-4 class engines. The two locomotives look very similar. The Mikado was a popular wheel arrangement on the B&O, with a total of 313 spread over 15 classes. Photo by Lloyd Wood, September 18, 1951

▶▶ Like most railroads in the 1930s, the B&O experimented with "streamlined" passenger trains in an attempt to satisfy the public's fascination with automobiles and airplanes. Most of the streamlined steam-power trains were built by adding sheet metal dressing to older locomotives. Streamlining rarely increased the locomotive's speed and often meant the engine weighed more than it did before streamlining. The *Royal Blue* was one of the road's streamlined steamers. Although the streamlining was impractical, there's no denying it looked good. Pacific (P-7 class) 5304 streaks westbound with its matching set of cars at Collingdale, Pa. Photo by Donald A. Summerville, 1940

In Philadelphia the B&O maintained several small yards, with railroad passengers using the B&O's own station located near the Pennsy's famed 30th Street Station.

Between Philadelphia and New York the railroad ran through an eclectic mix of open countryside, small towns, and big city industrial blight. Since the B&O was strictly a tenant along this stretch, it served virtually no industrial customers between Park Junction and the switching district it maintained in New York. The CNJ and Reading provided the Baltimore & Ohio with access to a high-speed corridor into the Big Apple and allowed the railroad to offer shippers a viable alternative to the Pennsy, right in the giant's back yard.

This important high-speed corridor offers tremendous visual contrast to the usual images of a mountain-climbing coal-hauler—images well worth preserving.

▲ The overcast skies accentuate the details in this moody shot of Wayne Junction in Philadelphia. The train threading its way through the junction is the *Capitol,* bound for D.C. from New York. The freight cars at left are spotted on the freight house tracks (the freight house is out of view to the left). The track at lower right is the Chestnut Hill branch. And don't miss that tank made out to look like a jar of Vicks Vapo-Rub! Photo by F. W. Trittenbach

▶ A stone's throw from the Reading's Wayne Junction Station in northwest Philadelphia, B&O trains use the Reading's four-track freight line, speeding to the Schuylkill River before turning south toward Philly's 24th Street and Chestnut Street Stations. The Washington-bound *Royal Blue* streaks by a CNJ freight. The two boxcars in the foreground are just as classic as the steam-powered streamliner. Photo by A. M. Rung, Jr.

◀◀ During and after World War II there was a boom in passenger traffic on the Philadelphia–Washington, D.C., corridor. The railroad added several fast express trains, like no. 45 shown here. The train is getting underway from Chestnut Street Station in Philadelphia. Its power is shiny Pacific no. 5309. Head-end business looks healthy. Note the wagontop boxcar, painted dark green and equipped with steam and signal lines for use in express service. Photo by A. M Rung, 1948

◀ The B&O made use of trackage rights on the Central Railroad of New Jersey through the Garden State. Here B&O train no. 5, the *Capitol Limited,* behind sleek EA no. 51, streaks past a westbound freight behind CNJ 2-8-2 no. 900 through Aldene, N.J. That skewed through truss bridge boosts the Lehigh Valley's main line over the CNJ. Photo by Theo Gay, June 29, 1946

◀ The sun highlights the glistening boiler jacket on 4-8-2 no. 5320 as she leads train no. 29 through Dunellen, N.J. It would be hard to find a shot showing a more "classic" heavyweight train. Photo by R. P. Morris, October 26, 1931

For years B&O passenger trains reached the Big Apple via a ferry connection at Jersey City, N.J. Competition from other railroads, not to mention the growth in highway and airline travel, rendered the B&O's service unprofitable. Here the *Royal Blue* leaves New York for the last time. This is the train's last run out of Jersey City. Photo by Don Wood, April 28, 1958

◀ Although the B&O provided passenger service between New York City and other points, B&O rails didn't actually extend into the Big Apple—at least for passenger trains. The farthest north you could travel on a B&O train was Jersey City, N.J., where the B&O was a tenant in the Central Railroad of New Jersey station. Buses and a ferry operated by the CNJ brought passengers across the Hudson into Manhattan. Here we see two B&O train buses delivering their passengers to New York. Photo by Wallace Abbey, August 27, 1953

▲ Number 195 was a one-of-a-kind boxcab diesel on the B&O roster, built in 1935 and assigned class DS-1A by the railroad. It spent most of its long life working switch jobs in New York City. Boxcar 268895 is also a classic, an M-26A class car, B&O's version of the numerous Pennsy X29s. And don't overlook the brick paving and the truck in the background. Photo was taken in B&O's 26th Street Yard in New York. Photo by Don Wood, June 1, 1956

Here, There, and Everywhere

Grafton, W.Va., sits deep in the heart of coal country. Grafton was truly a railroad town and was the heart of the B&O coal field lines. A trio of F units, led by no. 4503, departs town with a long coal train on one of those dreary, overcast days that seem prevalent in the mountains. Photo by J. W. Swanberg, March 30, 1959

Most of the photos in this volume show the Baltimore & Ohio as it was, a mainline railroad with high-speed freight service, challenging mountain grades assaulted by massive EM-1s and 2-10-2s, and a multi-track railroad linking many of the most important cities in the country. But there was more to the B&O than a massive rail system built on manifests and streamliners. This was also a railroad with branch lines and secondary routes, where a 2-8-0 or perhaps a Q class Mikado was considered "big" power. These same lines soldiered on in many cases into the diesel era, playing host to a single Geep or switcher.

West of Pittsburgh there was a series of small branch lines that terminated in places like Fairmont, West Virginia, and Butler, Mount Pleasant, and Boswell, Pennsylvania. The West Virginia coal country was also served by a series of small branch lines, most of which were worked by locals out of Grafton, W.Va., centerpiece of the railroad's coal lines. Many spots on the Monongah Division—especially those located south of Berkeley Run Junction—could easily be mistaken for a shortline railroad, as could the lines the Baltimore and Ohio acquired from the Buffalo & Susquehanna.

And while no one could ever mistake it for a short line, the Buffalo, Rochester & Pittsburgh, which was operated as the Buffalo Division of the B&O after 1932 between its three namesake cities, also seemed a little off the beaten path, at least when compared with the likes of Sand Patch and Jersey City.

Here then, in no particular order, is a photographic journey to some of the more remote spots on the B&O. They were all important and, I'm sure you'll agree, quite appealing in their own way.

▶ Railroading in West Virginia wasn't all mountain grades and big Mallets; there were also smaller branches served by smaller 2-8-0s and 4-6-0s. Looking like a scene created by a model railroader, Ten-Wheeler no. 2020 shoves train no. 457 across a wood trestle. Photo by Richard J. Cook, June 26, 1952

▶ below: A pair of Consolidations team up to handle an eastbound across the "million dollar" Pleasant Creek Viaduct between Grafton and Philippi, W.Va. The train is on the Charleston branch. The bridge was built by the U.S. Army Corps of Engineers as part of a dam construction project. Photo by A. O. Aldrich

▶▶ The Monongah Division reached deep into West Virginia hill country north and west of Grafton. This picturesque scene was at Haywood, W.Va. Number 4443 is heading for Fairmont with a coal extra from New Martinsville, W.Va. From Lumberport the line ran to Gaston Junction, where it joined the line to Fairmont. Photo by James P. Gallagher, 1956

◀ Level ground was hard to find in the B&O's eastern territories, often making it difficult to locate locomotive-servicing areas. The flat land formed by the confluence of the Monongahela River and Buffalo Creek provided an ideal spot for the Fairmont, W.Va., roundhouse and turntable. Several steamers, ready for their next assignments, are visible in this wonderful aerial shot. Photo by Martin Manning, August 6, 1946

▲ Although nearly a half-century old when photographed through the windshield of another classic in Genesee, Pa., Consolidation no. 3127 still looks almost new. The well-maintained 2-8-0 was one of 26 ex-Buffalo & Susquehanna locomotives built in 1908. Classified E-60 class by new owner B&O, the engines served faithfully until the end of steam in 1958. Photo by Philip R. Hastings

▲ It seems as though the engineer is giving the photographer a once-over as the little Consolidation hustles along with its Addison-to-Galeton freight on the Buffalo & Susquehanna subdivision. Freight car historians will note the differences between the two tank cars coupled to no. 3127's tank. The photographer caught the action on the B&S's twisting grade between Westfield and Sabinsville, Pa. Photo by Mike Runey

The Buffalo, Rochester & Pittsburgh became the Baltimore & Ohio's Buffalo Division on January 1, 1932. One of the most spectacular spots on the line was this bridge over the Allegheny River. The five-car train of matched heavyweights is no. 252, running between Pittsburgh and Buffalo. The power is 4-6-2 no. 5236, a P-6a built in 1922. Photo by Richard Cook, Sept. 3, 1954

CSX
Chessie System

The B&O Today

It may say "Chessie System" on its flanks but this is still a B&O locomotive and train. Each of the three component railroads kept its own identity under Chessie System, united with a common paint scheme. With the Grafton Hotel forming an unmistakable backdrop, B&O no. 3802 leads a long consist out of Grafton, West Virginia, ready once again to prove that horsepower can defeat gravity. Photo by Jay Potter, April 6, 1986

For many it's hard to believe that the Baltimore & Ohio of the late steam and early diesel years is two generations removed from the company that presently operates the lines originally conceived and built by the B&O. The beginning of the end for an independent B&O dates back as far as the early years of the 20th century when other railroads, primarily the Pennsylvania and Union Pacific, acquired significant quantities of B&O stock. But it wasn't until the 1960s that it became apparent that the B&O would become one of the increasing numbers of fallen flags.

In 1960 the Chesapeake & Ohio started acquiring large amounts of B&O stock—enough to control the railroad. Like the B&O, the C&O extended from the eastern seaboard into the Midwest. And like the B&O, the C&O was primarily a coal-hauling railroad. Although New York Central also made a bid for control of the B&O, the stockholders approved C&O control, a wise decision considering the eventual fate of NYC in the Penn Central debacle.

On May 1, 1962, B&O stockholders formally approved C&O control. The Interstate Commerce Commission approved the deal. By 1964 the C&O had acquired more than 90 percent of the outstanding

B&O stock. By 1967 the ICC allowed B&O and C&O control of the Western Maryland. (B&O's WM stock had been controlled for years by the B&O in the form of a non-voting trust.) Although operating patterns were changed, the B&O still held on to an independent corporate identity through this era—locomotives still said "B&O."

That changed on June 15, 1973, when the B&O, C&O, and WM were made subsidiaries of the newly created Chessie System. Still, the B&O retained some level of independence. Although there was wholesale abandonment of WM routes that duplicated B&O lines, the B&O itself remained relatively intact. Chessie System locomotives

The Chessie System railroads were eventually merged into CSX Transportation. Although the locomotives are far removed from the mighty articulateds that once hauled black diamonds out of the hollers, coal is still big business for CSX. Here's an eastbound CSX coal train on former C&O trackage near White Sulphur Springs, W.Va. Photo by John B. Corns, August 22, 1990

were painted a vivid paint scheme—bright yellow, blue, and vermilion. The railroad resurrected the C&O's famed kitten of the 1940s and '50s as its logo and name, including a stylized silhouette of Chessie herself inside the large "C." But the B&O was still an independent corporate entity, one of three subsidiary components of the new holding company. Cars, locomotives, and trains were identified with each company's reporting marks.

On May 1, 1983, the WM was formally merged into the Baltimore & Ohio. The B&O lasted as an independent corporate entity for four more years, until April 30, 1987, when it was merged into the C&O. Four months later the C&O was merged into CSX Transportation, a mega-railroad comprised of virtually every railroad in the southeast (except Norfolk & Western and

Southern, which themselves merged to form Norfolk Southern) and many in the Midwest.

Most recently, CSX has expanded even further, taking over half of Conrail. There are obviously many differences between the B&O's teakettles of old and even the mighty articulateds of a half century ago and the wide-nose diesel giants that dominate the former B&O today. Thanks to deregulation, improvements in operations and physical plant, and the booming economy, CSX and the other mega-railroads of today still provide a valuable service—the same one Charles Carroll and his countrymen needed almost two centuries ago: transporting raw material and finished goods from where they are to where they need to be as efficiently as possible. That, in its most basic essence, is railroading.

Although it's been almost 30 years since B&O paint started disappearing under Chessie yellow, there are still signs of the railroad all along the right-of-way. But the best, and most visible, evidence of the B&O and its importance to the growth of our nation can be found in the B&O Railroad Museum, located in the former Mount Clare Shops in Baltimore, Maryland. The museum boasts one of the country's best collection of vintage locomotives from the B&O and other railroads. The crown jewels of the collection are displayed inside the magnificent roundhouse, itself a rare gem of American railroad heritage. A pilgrimage to visit this collection is certainly a worthwhile journey for anyone interested in railroads or railroading.

Index of Photographs

Sand Patch Tunnel, 94
Silver Spring, Md., 33
Terra Alta, W.Va., 72, 73, 75, 78,
   80, 81
Wampum, Pa., 95
Washington, D.C., 30
West Newton, Pa., 105
White Sulphur Springs, W.Va., 125
Williamsport, Md., 100

Diesel locomotives
DS-1A 195, 115
E1 51, 113
E6 1411, 39
E7 70, 49
E8A 1440, 12
E8 152, 34
E8 85, 33
F3A 86, 28
FA-2 807, 53
F7 182, 51
F7 186, 69
F7 192, 63, 72

F7 281, 45
F7 949, 36
F7 4498, 31
F7 4503, 117
FT 1, 103
FT 5, 40, 46, 52
FT 105, 85
FT 7, 66
GP9 746, 19
GP9 741, 19
GP9 5960, 94
RDC-1, 24
SW1 201, 26
SW1 203, 27

Steam locomotives
0-4-0T 98, 17
2-8-0 3127, 121
2-8-0 4443, 119
2-8-2 4423, 78
2-8-2 4494, 108
2-10-2 6105, 96
2-10-2 6113, 56

2-10-2 6144, 50'
2-10-2 6145, 86
2-10-2 6200, 105
2-10-2 6209, 54
2-10-2 6222, 95
**** 7101, 61
0-8-8-0 7047, 76
0-8-8-0 7049, 76
2-8-8-0 7108, 82
2-8-8-0 7120, 104
2-8-8-0 7133, 64, 79, 82
2-8-8-0 7153, 79
2-8-8-0 7170, 74
2-8-8-4 7600, 101
2-8-8-4 7603, 80
2-8-8-4 7605, 81
2-8-8-4 7606, 67
2-8-8-4 7608, cover, 98
2-8-8-4 7609, 19, 20, 59
2-8-8-4 7613, 70
2-8-8-4 7614, 75, 97
2-8-8-4 7616, 100
2-8-8-4 7625, 38

4-6-0 2020, 118
4-6-2 5116, 22
4-6-2 5236, 123
4-6-2 5301, 44, 83
4-6-2 5304, 109
4-6-2 5309, 112
4-8-2 5320, 113
4-6-2 5806, 89
4-8-2 5051, 49
4-8-2 5566, 90
4-8-2 5662, 88
4-8-2 5572, 37
****4320, 32
****4615, 25

Passenger trains
Capitol Limited, 12, 107, 110, 113
Cincinnatian, 45, 60, 83
Cleveland Night Express, 43
Columbian, 42
Diplomat, 34
Washingtonian, 28, 58, 90
Royal Blue, 109, 111, 114